13 American Artists
Children Should Know

Brad Finger

PRESTEL
Munich · Berlin · London · New York

Contents

What makes an artist "American"? Many American artists were born outside the United States, and a few spent much of their lives in other countries! But most of them produced art that revealed something about being an American. Some painted famous American scenes—from giant city skyscrapers to vast prairie land. Others used their artworks to poke fun at the American way of life.

In this book, you will read about thirteen of the most important American artists. You will also see a few of their best creations. Some of the words in this book are followed by an asterisk,* because they may be hard to understand. A glossary at the back of the book will explain these words to you.

For each artist, you can follow a timeline that shows what was happening in the world when the person lived. There are also some quiz questions about the art that we show you. If you want to learn more about an artist, we provide tips for further reading, places to visit, and web addresses that will help you. We even have some good suggestions for how you can create your own American art—even if you're not an American!

Here you will find explanations of the technical terms!

Born:
February 24, 1836
in Boston,
Massachusetts

Died:
September 29, 1910
in Prout's Neck,
Maine

Lived in:
Boston, New York City,
Prout's Neck

Painting styles:
Realism,*
Impressionism*

Hobby:
Boating

Tip:
You can visit the home of Winslow Homer in Prout's Neck, Maine. Read about the home at the website www.portlandmuseum. org/about/homerstudio. shtml.

Winslow Homer — A Great American Traveler

His artwork showed how exciting and dramatic nature could be.

Winslow loved the outdoors and outdoor life. When he was a young man, he began working as an illustrator for magazines. He traveled around the country to find interesting people and places to draw.

In 1861, the Civil War* began in America. Winslow was sent to follow the United States army and to illustrate the soldiers' lives. His war drawings, which included many battle scenes, would appear in a magazine called *Harper*'s Weekly. They showed readers how difficult army life was for the young soldiers.

After the Civil War ended, Homer continued his travels. He especially enjoyed boating and hiking in remote, natural areas—places like the woodlands of Maine and the tropical coasts of the Bahamas.* Winslow captured the rough beauty of all these places in his art. He often used watercolor paints* to show how sunlight could make unusual colors at certain times of the day.

By the end of his life, Winslow had become one of the best-known American painters. His artworks promoted an independent lifestyle that many Americans admired.

Snap the Whip, 1872
The Butler Institute of American Art, Youngstown, Ohio

Try making your own outdoor work of art. You can draw what you find in your back yard, or in a local park. It's always good to get outside!

It's time to have some fun on a sunny day! In this painting, schoolchildren are taking a break from their lessons to play a game. What do you like to play outside?

The Adirondack Guide, 1894
Museum of Fine Arts,
Boston,
Bequest of
Mrs. Alma H. Wadleigh

Homer often traveled deep into the wilderness to find peace and happiness. This water-color shows a boating trip that he took in the Adirondack Mountains in New York State. Homer's rich, unusual colors make the forest look mysterious and remote, as if it is being discovered for the first time!

🌟 1874 The Impressionists hold their first art exhibition in Paris

Mary Cassatt 1844–1926

John Singer Sargent 1856–1925

1871 France is defeated by Prussia in the Franco-Prussian War 🌟
1861–1865 American Civil War 🌟

1887 The Eiffel Tower is completed 🌟
for the Paris World's Fair

🌟 1893 The

1840   1845   1850   1855   1860   1865   1870   1875   1880   1885   1890   1895

Born:
  May 22, 1844
  in Allegheny City,
  Pennsylvania
Died:
  June 14, 1926
  in Mesnil-Theribus,
  France
Lived in:
  Allegheny City, Paris,
  Mesnil-Theribus
Painting styles:
  Impressionism*

Mary Cassatt— An American Woman in Paris

In an era dominated by men, Cassatt made art about the lives of women.

Mary Cassatt was a restless person. She grew up in a wealthy American family that liked to move around—her childhood was spent in France and Germany as well as the United States. Mary knew from an early age that she wanted to become an artist. But the schools in America didn't teach her everything she needed to know. So in 1865, she moved to Paris, the capital of the art world. There she learned to become a great painter.

Cassatt admired a new group of French artists called the Impressionists.* Their paintings looked as restless as she was, using blotches of color to show how light could shine on a city street or country field. Cassatt also painted the effects of light. But her art focused on people, and especially women. She loved to portray young mothers taking care of their children; and she depicted women sewing, bathing, and doing other activities of ordinary life.

Throughout her career, Cassatt never stopped moving around and learning new things. She traveled to Spain, Italy, and Egypt; and she even created a way of making pictures that looked like Japanese woodblock prints.* Mary also taught people about art. She helped make Impressionism popular in the United States, convincing many wealthy Americans to buy Impressionist art for their own collections and for art museums. This style of art—and the art of Mary Cassatt—remain popular today.

The Child's Bath, 1893
The Art Institute of Chicago

Cassatt painted women at work, especially those who raised children. In the 1800s, women started caring for children in new ways. For example, they began to understand the value of regular bathing. This painting shows how children were bathed in Mary's time.

Young Girl Reading, 1894
Hirshhorn Museum, Washington DC

The girl is absorbed in her reading—she doesn´t even seem to notice that she´s being painted. Cassatt has drawn her face in careful detail, but her robe has been quickly sketched in bold colors

Good to know:
Mary Cassatt was a close friend of Edgar Degas, the famous French Impressionist painter. Degas even painted Mary's portrait!

Suggestion for further reading:
Mary Cassatt: *Family Pictures* by Jane O'Connor

Breakfast in Bed, 1897
Virginia Steele Scott Collection
San Marino, California

Cassatt understood the close bond between parent and child. She portrayed that bond in unusual ways, as in this scene of a mother and child eating breakfast. Such pictures were unusual in the 1800s, because most people did not want to be painted in their bed clothes!

1860s The Gilded Age of economic growth begins in America ✳

John Singer Sargent 1856–1925
Mary Cassatt 1844–1926

✳ 1876 The United States celebrates its
Centennial, or 100th anniversary

✳ 1861–1865 American Civil War

| 1840 | 1845 | 1850 | 1855 | 1860 | 1865 | 1870 | 1875 | 1880 | 1885 | 1890 | 1895 |

Madame X, 1884
The Metropolitan Museum
of Art, New York

Sargent could capture
his subject's personalities.
This famous painting,
called Madame X, shows
a wealthy American
named Virginie Gautreau.
She became famous
in Paris for her beauty.
Sargent gives her an
expression and pose
that portrays her self-
confident, almost dramatic
nature. He also uses the
rich black colors in her
dress to highlight her
beautiful, pale skin.

Good to know:
Sargent painted the
portraits of two
American Presidents:
Theodore Roosevelt
and Woodrow Wilson.

John Singer Sargent— Painter of Wealth

America was becoming a prosperous country in the 1800s, and Sargent painted the people and lifestyles of this "gilded age."*

Born:
    January 12, 1856
    in Florence, Italy
Died:
    April 15, 1925
    in London
Lived in:
    Florence; Nice, France;
    Dresden, Germany;
    Paris; London
Painting styles:
    Realism*
Hobby:
    Traveling

He was an American painter who rarely visited the United States. Sargent came from a wealthy family, and he spent his career surrounded by wealthy people. As a boy, John traveled with his family from one European country to another. So when it came time for him to choose a career, he decided to study painting in Paris.

Sargent soon became one of the best portrait artists in the world. He painted the rich and famous of his day, many of whom were Americans like himself—living or traveling away from their own country. John was especially good at painting women. He knew how to capture the perfect expression on a face, and he used quick brushstrokes and rich colors to portray his sitters' elegant clothes and expensive furniture.

When he was in his fifties, Sargent began depicting other kinds of subjects. He painted landscapes while traveling in America, and he even portrayed soldiers fighting in France during World War I. But his realistic, energetic style of painting never changed. Sargent also remained an American abroad—dying in London in 1925.

Edward Hopper 1882–1967

1914–1918 First World War

1929 The U.S. Stock M

Mark Rothko 1903–1970

Alexander Calder 1898–1976

1920s The Jazz Age, a period of exciting new music and culture

1929–1941 The Great D

1880   1885   1890   1895   1900   1905   1910   1915   1920   1925   1930   1935

Born:
July 22, 1882
in Nyack, New York

Died:
May 15, 1967
in New York City

Lived in:
Nyack, New York City,
South Truro (MA)

Painting style:
Realism*

Hobby:
Reading

Suggestion for further reading:
Edward Hopper:
Summer at the Seashore
by Deborah Lyons
(Prestel Publishing)

Edward Hopper— An Independent Artist

Hopper didn't follow trends. He was a modern artist who worked in an old-fashioned way. But his quiet and some-times sad paintings tell us a lot about modern America.

Edward almost didn't become a great artist. He learned to paint as a child, but he did not come from a rich family. So to earn money, he spent years making illustrations for magazines. Hopper disliked this work. His bosses were always telling him what to draw—and he wanted to make art that interested him.

So when Edward wasn't working on illustrations, he slowly, carefully developed his own painting style. Many artists who were Hopper's age made "modern" paintings, which showed people and things in an unreal manner. But Edward preferred to paint the real world as he saw it. He liked to show the way light shines on people and objects—and how it creates beautiful patterns. He also liked to show how modern America could be a lonely and unhappy place. Many people in Hopper's art seem bored; even if they are doing fun things like going to the moves or eating in restaurants. Hopper also gave "personalities" to the buildings and landscapes that he painted, often making them look as sad and isolated as his people.

By the time Hopper was in his forties, his hard work began to pay off. More and more people noticed the beauty in Edward's sad images, and more and more bought his paintings. Today, Hopper is among the most beloved of all American artists.

Rooms by the Sea, 1951
Yale University Art Gallery,
New Haven, Connecticut

Does anybody live here? Hopper uses light to give this picture a feeling of loneliness. Sunshine floods into the house, but it reveals a barren wall and an empty room. Even the house's location looks remote—almost as though it is floating in the middle of the ocean!

Nighthawks, 1942
The Art Institute of Chicago

Hopper's most famous painting is called Nighthawks. The customers in this diner don't look happy. One man sits all alone; while the couple stares straight ahead, barely noticing each other. Outside the diner, the harsh city lights shine on an empty street corner.

Quiz:
Why is this picture entitled *Nighthawks*?

1912 New Mexico becomes a U.S. state
Georgia O`Keeffe 1887–1986

1914–1918 First World War

Edward Hopper 1882–1967

Alexander Calder 1898–1976
1927 Charles Lindberg makes the first non-stop flight from America to Europe

1880   1885   1890   1895   1900   1905   1910   1915   1920   1925   1930   1935

Born:
November 15, 1887
near Sun Prairie,
Wisconsin

Died:
March 6, 1986
in Santa Fe,
New Mexico

Lived in:
Sun Prairie, New
York City, Amarillo
(TX), Columbia (SC),
Abiquiu (NM)

Art style:
Abstract art,*
Expressionism*

Hobby:
Pottery making

Georgia O`Keeffe— The American Landscape

She painted the world as a living place. Even things like desert mountains and old churches came to life in her art.

Throughout her life, Georgia O'Keeffe would spend hours walking out-doors and looking for beautiful things. Sometimes a tiny flower would catch her eye. Other times she would notice the curve of a giant mountain peak. She captured all of these things in her paintings.

Georgia began to draw and paint nature as a little girl. But it took her many years to develop her own style. In the 1910s, when she was living in New York City, she made her first abstract* paintings. Abstract art focuses on shapes and colors that don't represent things in real life. By creating this kind of art, Georgia learned to make simple shapes in an expressive and beautiful way.

Soon, she began using abstract techniques to paint nature. She started with flowers. Georgia would look carefully at a flower to find beautiful shapes within it. She would then paint these individual shapes on a large canvas,* often using brilliant colors to make the shapes come to life. People soon admired Georgia's new art, and she became famous.

Later in her life, O'Keeffe moved from New York City to a desert ranch in New Mexico, in the American Southwest. There she discovered new things to paint. She found barren, colorful desert mountains that looked like reclining animals; she found old adobe* churches with sleek walls and tiny windows; and she even noticed animal skulls scattered on the sandy ground. Georgia remained in New Mexico for the rest of her life. But the popularity of her art spread around the world.

City Night, 1926
The Minneapolis
Institute of Arts

As a young woman,
Georgia spent many years
painting in New York
City. This picture is her
impression of huge New
York skyscrapers at night.
Seen from the ground,
the buildings create a
deep, barren canyon in
the middle of the city.

Tip:
You can learn more about
this artist by visiting the
Georgia O'Keeffe Museum
in Santa Fe, New Mexico.
It has many of Georgia's
most famous paintings.
For more information
about the museum,
visit the website
www.okeefemuseum.org.

Iris (Dark Iris I), 1927
Colorado Springs
Fine Arts Center

Georgia O'Keeffe could make nature seem romantic. This picture of an iris shows the flower's soft, flowing shapes, almost like the shapes of a fancy dress. Delicate colors add to the painting's beauty.

Good to know:
O'Keeffe's New Mexico home was near an ancient Native American town called Taos Pueblo. The buildings of this town are made of dried earth called adobe, and they are hundreds of years old. Georgia made paintings of Taos Pueblo.

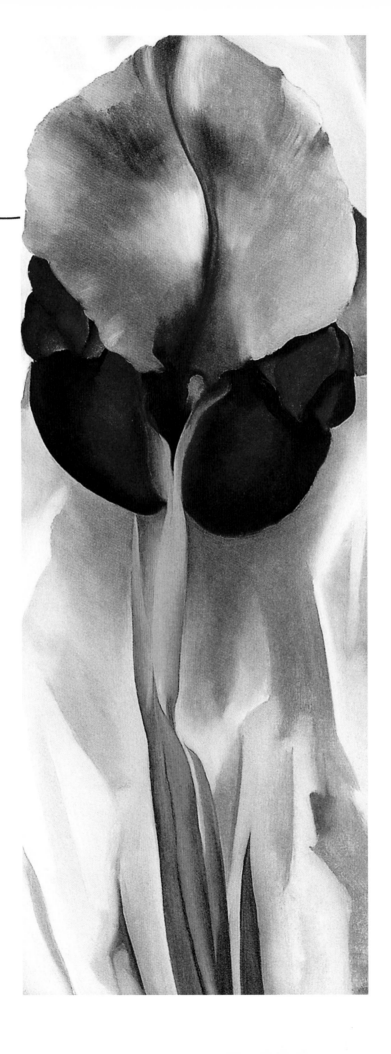

The Cliff Chimneys, 1938
Milwaukee Art Museum

O'Keeffe often painted the barren desert landscape of New Mexico. But her images aren't exactly true to life. She changed the shapes of rocks and mountains, often making them look like living things. Notice the base of this huge cliff. It almost resembles a crouching animal!

Born:
> July 22, 1898
> in Lawnton,
> Pennsylvania

Died:
> November 11, 1976
> in New York City

Lived in:
> Lawnton, Pasadena
> (CA), San Francisco,
> New York City, Paris

Art style:
> Surrealism*

Children:
> Sandra, Mary

Interests:
> Theater, Dance

Good to know:
One of Calder's first creations was an entire miniature circus—complete with lions, clowns, and trapeze artists! All of these circus characters were attached to wires. Alexander could "perform" circus acts by moving them around, almost like a puppeteer moves puppets.

Alexander Calder — Art in Motion

His twisting, fluttering mobiles showed that great art didn't have to stand still.

Alexander loved things that moved. When he was eleven years old, Calder made a metal duck that could move back and forth when you tapped it on the head. He gave this duck to his parents as a Christmas present!

Calder spent the rest of his life creating moving works of art. As a young man, he settled in Paris, then the center of the art world. He quickly made friends with famous French painters and sculptors. Calder often fashioned movable portraits of his friends out of twisted wire!

Around the year 1930, he became interested in the movement of simple shapes. Calder cut pieces of metal into thin, curved forms that could twist easily in the air. He then attached these thin pieces to a "skeleton" of metal wires. When the wire skeleton was hung from the ceiling or placed on a stand, the individual pieces—and sometimes the whole sculpture—could move in different directions. Calder's artist friends soon gave these creations a name: mobiles.

Alexander's mobiles became well known, and he produced them in many different materials and shapes. Later in his life, he started making large sculptures called stabiles for city squares and parks. The stabiles are designed carefully so that their big, curving bodies can rest on thin legs without falling over. Because they are constructed this way, many Calder stabiles seem as energetic as his moving art. Some even look like huge monsters that could pounce on unsuspecting passers-by!

Four Leaves and Three Petals, 1939
Musée national d'art moderne, Centre Georges Pompidou, Paris

This plant-like mobile rests on a thin metal stand. Notice the three tiny shapes at the top of the sculpture. They are designed to resemble flower petals, and their bright colors make them stand out from the rest of the piece.

Tip:
You can go to the website www.calder.org to look at more pictures of Calder's art, and to see old photographs of the artist at work.

1914–1918 First World War   1918–1940 Lativa is an independent country for a short time   1945 The United State
Mark Rothko 1903–1970

Jackson Pollock 1912–1956

1929 The Great Depression   1939–1945 Second World War

1910   1915   1920   1923   1926   1930   1933   1936   1940   1943   1946   1950

Born:
September 25, 1903
in Daugavpils, Latvia

Died:
February 25, 1970
in New York City

Lived in:
Daugavpils, Portland
(OR), New York City

Painting style:
Abstract
Expressionism*

Children:
Kate, Christopher

Mark Rothko— Painting of the Mind

Rothko's paintings may appear simple at first—just a bunch of colored rectangles. But the more you look at them, the more mysterious and complex they become!

No matter how hard he worked, Mark could never please himself. He immigrated* to America from Latvia at the age of ten, but he had a hard time making friends in his new country. He felt like a foreigner who never fit in.

Mark tried many different jobs as a young man. He worked in a clothing factory, and he even tried to become an actor! When these jobs didn't work out, he started painting. But he could never find his own style.

In the 1940s, the United States fought in World War II. America and its allies won the war, but beautiful cities were destroyed and millions of innocent people were killed. When the war ended in 1945, Mark and other artists began to create new styles of painting for a changed world. Rothko's new art featured rectangles of different, carefully chosen colors. The rectangles were placed one on top of the other, and they had unusual, fuzzy edges. Many people found the shapes to be relaxing, like floating clouds. Others thought they resembled violent forces of nature, like earthquakes. Rothko let people come up with their own ideas about his work.

Mark Rothko had finally become a famous painter, but he would never be content with himself. He committed suicide in 1970.

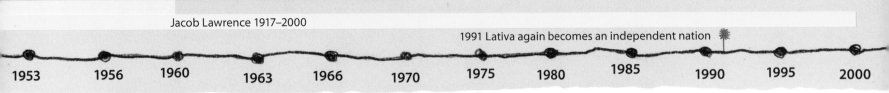

No. 10, 1950
The Museum of Modern Art, New York

Rothko's famous rectangular shapes appear to float on the canvas.* What do you think about when you look at this painting?

Good to know:
At the end of his life, Rothko decorated an entire chapel in Houston, Texas. He made many abstract* paintings for this project. You can read more about the chapel at http://www.rothkochapel.org.

1927 *The Jazz Singer* is released, the first important film with sound

Joseph Cornell 1903–1972

Mark Rothko 1903–1970

Jacob Lawrence 1917–2000

1924 The Surrealist art movement is founded in Paris

1929–1941 The Great Depression

1939–1945 Second World War

1905   1910   1915   1920   1925   1930   1935   1940   1945   1950   1955   1960

Object (Roses des Vents), 1942–1953

The Museum of Modern Art, New York

Whenever you opened up one of Joseph Cornell's boxes, you found a colorful treasure inside! Look at all the tiny maps—and pieces of maps—that can be found in this artwork. What else do you see here?

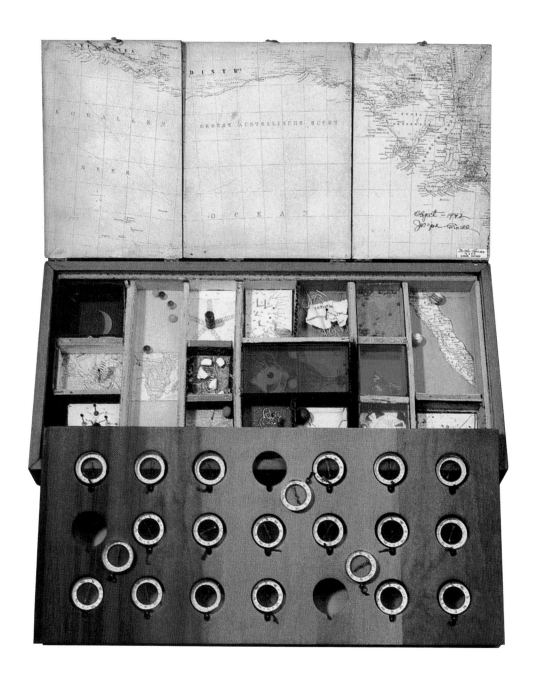

Try making your own collage box. You might use an old shoe box and fill it with things you have collected. Make sure to arrange your things creatively. You can even color parts of the box to make your collage look more interesting!

Joseph Cornell— Artist and Collector

Cornell made art out of ordinary—and sometimes strange—objects that he found and kept.

Do you like to collect things? Maybe you have a box of postcards in your closet or a family of dolls under your bed? Joseph Cornell was a collector as well, and he did more than just keep things in his room. He used them to create his own unique kind of artwork.

Joseph was interested in all forms of art—painting, theater, dance, and even movies. When he saw an artwork that he liked, he always kept a little souvenir to remember what he had seen. Sometimes it was a program from a play. Other times it was a reproduction of a painting. Soon his collection of objects grew, and he began to arrange them in collages.* Cornell would place the objects in special boxes, putting certain objects next to others in unusual ways.

In the 1930s, Joseph began showing his boxes to other people, especially artists known as Surrealists.* The Surrealists were making artworks similar to Cornell's—taking ordinary things and showing them in a way that gave them new meaning. Joseph soon became a respected artist himself, and his collages became more and more elaborate as he got older.

Cornell even used his love of collecting to make his own movies. He would take pieces of old movie film and put them back together in a strange— and often funny—manner.

Born:
December 24, 1903
in Nyack, New York
Died:
December 29, 1972
in Flushing,
New York City
Lived in:
Nyack, New York City
Painting style:
Surrealism*
Hobby:
Watching movies

Louise Bourgeois 1911-2010

1925 Worlds Fair is held in Paris

Andy Warhol 1928–1987

Jasper Johns is born 1930

1939–1945 Second World War

1910   1915   1920   1925   1930   1935   1940   1945   1950   1952   1954   1956

Born:
December 25, 1911
in Paris

Died:
May 31, 2010
in New York City

Lived in:
Paris, New York City

Art style:
Surrealism,*
Post-modernism*

Sons:
Michel, Jean-Louis,
Alain

Louise Bourgeois— Materials and Memories

Her sculptures often represent people and memories from long ago—and Bourgeois lived a long life!

Louise Bourgeois never forgot her childhood. She grew up in France, the daughter of artistic parents. Both her mother and father repaired old woven pictures called tapestries.* Young Louise helped her parents in their work, but her childhood wasn't easy. Her father was unfaithful to her mother, and there was always tension in the family.

Louise began her own career in the arts at a young age. She studied drawing, painting, and sculpture, but it would take her many years before she became successful. While still in Paris, she married an American named Robert Goldwater, a teacher of art history. Together, they moved to New York City.

Bourgeois slowly developed a style of sculpture that was uniquely her own. She used simple materials such as rubber, wood, metal, and fabric to create images with many complex meanings. Her most famous works are huge spider-like sculptures called "Maman," many of which stand outdoors. For Louise, they represent characteristics she saw in her mother. Spiders weave and mend webs, just like her mother wove and mended tapestries—and tried to mend problems in her family. Spiders are also delicate creatures that show how fragile life can be.

Bourgeois' life was an unusually long one. She died at age ninety-eight in New York City, her adopted American home.

**Spiral Woman,
1951–1952**
The Museum of
Modern Art, New York

Louise often usesd simple
materials and interesting
shapes in her artwork.
This sculpture is meant
to represent a woman.
Look closely at the spiral-
shaped wooden part.
Does it resemble a twist-
ing dress—or something
else? What do you think?

Good to know:
Copies of Bourgeois'
famous *Maman*
sculptures appear
in museums around
the world—in such
countries as Canada,
Cuba, France, Russia,
South Korea, Spain, and
the United States!

Maman, 1999
Private Collection, courtesy
Cheim & Ried, New York

Bourgeois' giant spider
sculptures look almost
like dinosaur skeletons.
These steel and marble
creations were designed
when Louise was nearly
ninety years old!

You can make your own artwork about something from the
past. Maybe you have an object that reminds you of a vacation
that you took with your family—an old toy, perhaps?
Try making a drawing of that toy and see if it helps you
remember more about your vacation.

1948 The state of Israel is founded

Jackson Pollock 1912–1956

Jacob Lawrence 1917–2000

Andy Warhol 1928–1987

1929–1941 The Great Depression   1939–1945 Second World War

1900   1905   1910   1915   1920   1925   1930   1935   1940   1945   1950   1955

Born:
January 28, 1912
in Cody, Wyoming
Died:
August 11, 1956
in East Hampton,
New York
Lived in:
Chico (CA); New York
City; East Hampton
Painting style:
Abstract
Expressionism*

Jackson Pollock—Drip Painter

He showed that art did not have to be made standing still!

Jackson Pollock didn't like obeying rules. As a teen-ager, he was kicked out of school many times. When he decided to become a painter, he first tried to paint scenes of American life. But this style wasn't right for him. Pollock didn't even like the way painters normally made their art—standing or sitting calmly in front of an easel.* Pollock was a restless, energetic person who needed to find a different way to paint.

In the 1940s, when Pollock was in his thirties, he began to paint on huge canvases that were placed flat on the ground. Instead of making ordinary brushstrokes, he would move around the canvas—almost like a dancer—and would wave a paint-filled brush over the white surface. The paint would then drip from the brush and fall in colored lines on the canvas; lines that followed Jackson's own movements. Pollock would do these movements over and over again, covering the canvas with paint. The final result was an exciting mix of colors and lines, a picture that showed just how much energy and effort Pollock had put into making it.

Pollock's "drip" paintings soon made him famous. He became part of a group of New York artists called Abstract Expressionists.* All of these artists used abstract* shapes to "express" their feelings and personalities. Pollock, however, never got used to being famous. He died in a car crash at the young age of forty-four.

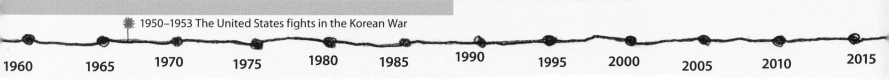

1950–1953 The United States fights in the Korean War

1960   1965   1970   1975   1980   1985   1990   1995   2000   2005   2010   2015

Pollock painted like an athlete! He danced around the canvas with his brush and let the paint drip onto the surface.

Good to know: Pollock created many of his artworks in a small barn in East Hampton, New York. This barn gave him lots of space—enough to perform his drip painting technique.

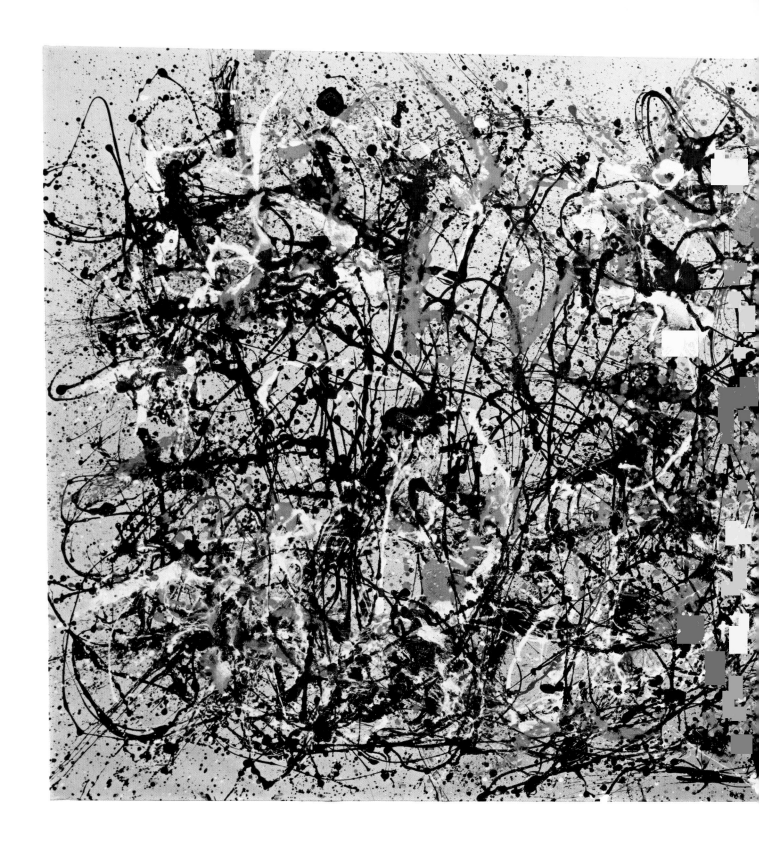

Autumn Rhythm No. 30, 1950
The Metropolitan Museum of Art, New York

A Jackson Pollock "drip" painting may appear messy at first glance. But if you look at it more carefully, you will notice how individual lines swirl in different directions around the canvas. You might even find hidden shapes in the painting. What do you see here?

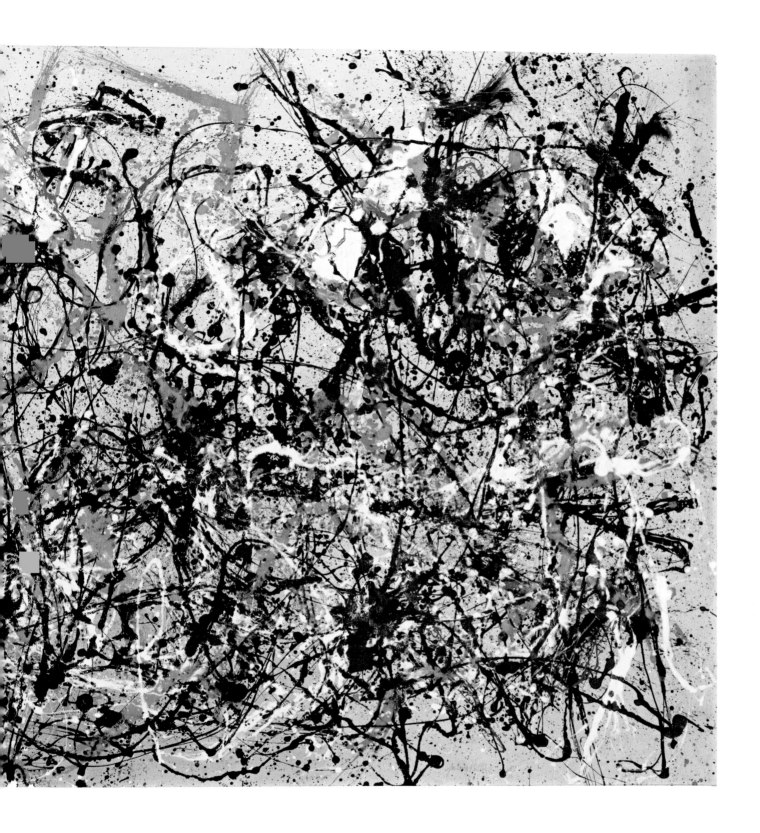

1910s–1920s Thousand of African Americans move to northern U.S. cities to find work

Jacob Lawrence 1917–2000

Andy Warhol 1928–1987

Jasper Johns is born 1930   1950s–1960s African Americans gain civil rights,

1939–1945 Second World War   including the right to go to schools o

1915   1920   1925   1930   1935   1940   1945   1948   1950   1953   1956   1960

The Migration Series/28. The labor agent who had been sent South by Northern industry was a very familiar person in the Negro counties, 1941 The Museum of Modern Art, New York

In the early 1900s, many African Americans had to travel a long way from home to find work. They moved from farms in the southern United States to big city factories in the north. Lawrence's paintings showed how difficult their journey was. In this picture, seven men wait in line to see if the man in the black hat has jobs for them.

Jacob Lawrence— The Art of Struggle

Lawrence's paintings show people who have had to work hard to survive—just like he did in his own life.

Born:
September 7, 1917 in Atlantic City, New Jersey
Died:
June 9, 2000 in Seattle, Washington
Lived in:
Atlantic City, New York City, Seattle
Painting style:
Cubism*, Expressionism*

Jacob grew up in an exciting place. His African American neighborhood in Harlem, New York City, was full of interesting people—jazz* musicians, dancers, actors, writers, and artists. But he also lived with people who had to struggle to support themselves. African Americans suffered discrimination in the United States. Many could not attend good schools or get good jobs. To make matters worse, young Jacob lived during the Great Depression of the 1930s, when every American was having a hard time finding work.

Jacob knew early on that he wanted to become an artist, and he quickly developed his own style. His paintings use vivid colors and simple shapes to represent people and objects—somewhat like the style of modern artists called Cubists.* But Jacob also wanted his art to show the lives and hardships of African Americans in the United States. He portrayed workers who were on the move, constantly looking for a better life. He also depicted people who constructed buildings or cleaned clothes; people who were often forgotten or overlooked.

Lawrence eventually became a professor of art in Seattle, Washington. Yet his expressive, colorful painting style never changed. Nor did he lose interest in the lives of people who struggle.

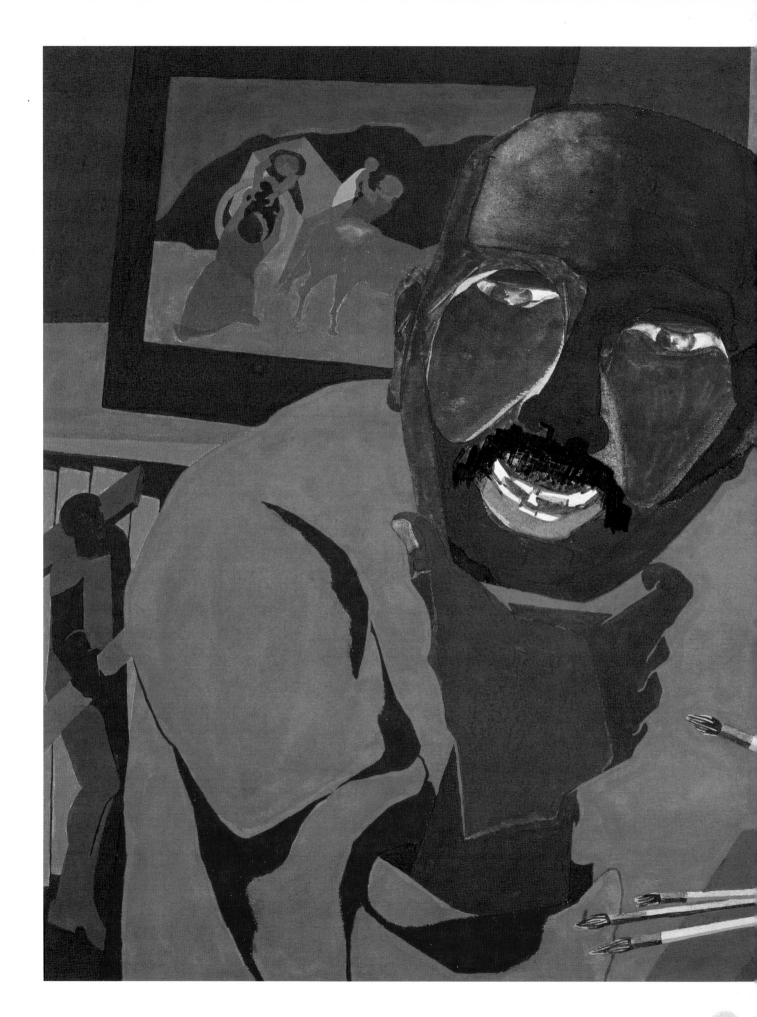

Self-portrait, 1977
National Academy of
Design, New York

Lawrence used simple
shapes to create the
heads and bodies of
his human figures. This
picture is a happy self-
portrait of the artist.

Good to know:
Jacob Lawrence made
a series of paintings
about the life of Toussaint
L'Ouverture. Toussaint,
who had been a slave
early in his life, helped
found the Caribbean
nation of Haiti in 1804.
Haiti was the first
country in the world
to be founded by
black people who
had been slaves.

Quiz:
Lawrence's self-portrait
shows many of the tools
that he used as a painter.
How many can you find?

Andy Warhol—The Art of Fame

He is one of the best-known American artists—and he wanted it that way!

Born:
August 6, 1928
in Pittsburgh,
Pennsylvania
Died:
February 22, 1987
in New York City
Lived in:
Pittsburgh, New York
City
Art style:
Pop Art*

Would you like to become famous? Andy Warhol once said, "In the future everybody will be world famous for fifteen minutes." He made sure that his own fame lasted much longer! As a young man, Andy made illustrations for magazine and newspaper advertisements. He liked the look of the shiny, colorful products that American businesses liked to sell. So he decided to include these "popular" images in his own paintings. One of his early works showed row upon row of Campbell's soup cans. This humorous picture helped begin an artistic movement called "Pop Art."*

Andy soon realized that celebrities, too, were "products" that could be marketed. The death of American actress Marilyn Monroe in 1962 inspired him to make a "portrait" of her. He took an old photograph and—in a process called silkscreen printing*—reproduced it many times on a large canvas.* This made Marilyn's image look like a soup can: something to be copied and sold.

People admired Warhol's early work, and Andy became a celebrity in his own right. He soon thought of other ways to combine art and popular culture. He began making his own movies in which the "actors" had to behave just as they would in real life. These movies show how simple human movements can be expressive. Warhol also promoted other artists, including the painter Jean-Michel Basquiat and the rock band The Velvet Underground. By the time Andy died in 1987, the desire for "fifteen minutes" of fame had become an important part of American culture.

Andy Warhol 1928–1987

🌸 1963 U.S. President John F. Kennedy is assassinated

1964–1975 The United States is involved in the Vietnam War
🌸 1969 First man on the moon

1947–1991 The Cold War

1940   1943   1946   1950   1955   1960   1965   1970   1975   1980   1985   1990

Sixteen Jackies, 1964
Walker Art Center, Minneapolis

Warhol was interested in famous people who experienced sadness in their lives. This artwork is a portrait of Jacqueline Kennedy. Her husband, U.S. President John F. Kennedy, was shot and killed in 1963. Look at the top and bottom rows of photographs. They show Mrs. Kennedy before the shooting. The photos in the middle rows were taken after the President was shot. How does this picture make you feel?

Tip:
To learn more about Warhol, you can visit the Andy Warhol museum in Pittsburgh, Pennsylvania. Read about the museum at the website www.warhol.org.

Make your own Pop Art. You might create a collage out of old cereal boxes. Cut out colorful pictures from the cereal boxes and glue them onto a piece of paper. You can also make your own colored drawings on the collage. Make sure you use your creativity!

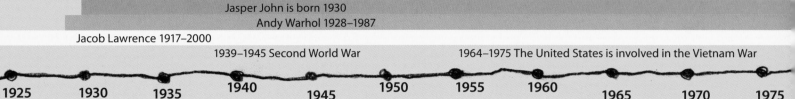
Jasper John is born 1930
Andy Warhol 1928–1987
Jacob Lawrence 1917–2000
1939–1945 Second World War   1964–1975 The United States is involved in the Vietnam War
1920   1925   1930   1935   1940   1945   1950   1955   1960   1965   1970   1975

Flag, 1954–55
The Museum of
Modern Art, New York

This is no ordinary
American flag. Look
closely—do you see some
unusual colors and
patterns in the stars and
stripes? Underneath
the paint layers lie bits
of newspaper and
other materials.

Tips for further reading:
Where is Jasper Johns?
by Debra Pearlman
(a Prestel publication)

Quiz:
Look closely at the
painting *Ventriloquist*.
At the left side of the
picture, Jasper Johns
painted something on
the door. Can you see
what it is?

Jasper Johns— Symbols and Surface

His unique American flags showed people how to see art in new ways.

Born:
May 15, 1930 in Augusta, Georgia
Lives in:
Connecticut
Painting style:
Jasper Johns does not believe his art belongs to any style, though some people call it Post-modernist art.*
Interests:
Music, Dance

The American flag is meant to symbolize the United States—and the lives and values of its people. It is an iconic* image that everybody recognizes. Japer Johns was always fascinated by iconic things, and he used them in his paintings.

As a young man in the 1940s, Johns moved from a small town in South Carolina to study painting in New York City, the capital of art at that time. Jasper struggled to find his own style. He was so upset with his early artworks that he destroyed most of them! Soon, however, he discovered artistic ways of painting the American flag and other symbolic images.

Johns' American flags seem simple at first glance. But if you look closely, you'll see that he used lots of different materials to create his image. First he glued bits of newspapers and other things over the canvas.* He then applied paint over this collage* of materials to create the final image. Johns' unusual technique gave his flags a mysterious, almost rough, appearance. It also made people notice and appreciate how an artist creates his art.

Ventriloquist, 1983
The Museum of Fine Arts, Houston

This Jasper Johns painting combines American flags with other ordinary objects. But not everything is quite right here. The two flags in the middle are the wrong colors—and the cups and bowls seem to be floating in mid-air! Why do you think the artist painted in this manner?

Glossary

ABSTRACT ART is a style of painting that uses shapes, lines, and other "abstract" forms that do not represent real things.

ABSTRACT EXPRESSIONISM is a type of abstract art. Abstract Expressionists use unreal forms and unusual colors to "express," or show, their thoughts and feelings.

ADOBE is a material used to make buildings in hot, dry places. People create adobe by mixing clay, straw, and other substances with water—and then letting the mixture dry in the sun. Adobe is strong and lasts a long time. It also keeps buildings cool in hot climates.

BAHAMAS is a group of islands in the Caribbean Sea. Together, the islands form a single, independent country.

CANVAS is a strong type of fabric on which artists make paintings. Canvases often come stretched out on a wooden frame.

CIVIL WAR IN AMERICA was fought between the United States and a group of former U.S. states from the South. This group, called the Confederate States of America (or the Confederacy), had left the United States in 1861—mostly over the issue of slavery. The northern states wanted to abolish slavery. But the southern states wanted to keep their African American slaves, many of whom worked on large southern farms called plantations. When the bloody Civil War ended in 1865, the Confederacy was defeated. Eventually, all the Confederate states rejoined the United States.

COLLAGE is a type of art in which different objects are placed together in a particular way to make a single image. Many collages combine things that don't normally belong together.

CUBISM is a style of painting that shows people and objects "broken up" into geometric shapes. Sometimes, Cubists portray an object from several different angles at the same time.

EASEL is a stand on which painters place their canvases when they paint. Many easels are made of wood.

EXPRESSIONISM is an art style that began during the early 1900s. Artists that work in this style use their art to "express," or show, their feelings and ideas. Expressionists do not portray things exactly as they appear in real life. Instead, they change the shapes of these things; and they often use bold, unrealistic colors.

GILDED AGE is a period in U.S. history that occurred from 1865 to the beginning of the 1900s. During that time, the country's economy grew rapidly, and many Americans became very wealthy. The word "gilded" refers to something that is covered in gold—or very expensive!

ICON is a well-known symbol. A picture of the American flag, for example, is an iconic image that symbolizes the United States.

IMMIGRANT is a person who moves from one country in order to make a new home in another country. During the late 1800s and early 1900s, thousands of people from Europe immigrated to the United States. Many moved to America to find work, while others fled their countries to escape governments that were taking away their freedom.

IMPRESSIONISM is a style of painting that developed in France in the 1860s. Impressionists created personal "impressions" of what they had seen in real life. They used color to show how light shone on objects at a particular moment of the day or season of the year.

INCENSE is a mixture of wood and other plant materials that have a nice smell when burnt. People in North Africa, the Middle East, and other parts of the world have long burned incense during religious ceremonies. They often do so using beautiful metal containers called incense burners.

JAZZ is a kind of music and dance developed by African Americans in the early 1900s. Jazz is known, in part, for its complicated and exciting rhythms.

MOORISH ARCHITECTURE is a style of building that developed in North Africa more than 1,000 yeas ago. The word "Moor" is sometimes used to refer to people in North Africa. The most famous type of Moorish architecture is the mosque, or Islamic religious building. It features beautiful, horseshoe-shaped arches.

POP ART "Pop" stands for "popular," and Pop Artists typically show people and things that are well-loved and easily understood. For example, they may portray comic book scenes, movie stars, or even soup cans!

POST-MODERNISM means "after Modernism." From the 1920s through the 1950s, Modernism was the most important style of art. Some of the best-known Modernists used unrealistic, abstract* styles. During the 1950s, however, young artists began making new works that looked different from Modernist art. Many of these "Post-modernists" decided to paint real people and objects again.

REALISM is a style of art that tries to portray people and things as they appear in real life. For example, realist painters make people and objects—as well as spaces—look three-dimensional.

SILKSCREEN is a technique used to make both paintings and prints. In this technique, an artist will apply a piece of silk to a canvas. The artist will then let paint or ink seep through the silk and onto the canvas surface.

SURREALISM is an art style that takes familiar objects and presents them in an unfamiliar way. Some Surrealists combine things that don't normally go together. Others try to give new meanings to ordinary objects. Surrealist artworks often seem mysterious, dreamlike, or even funny.

TAPESTRY is a kind of woven picture. People have been making tapestries for centuries, often using wool, cotton, or silk. Many older tapestries are quite large, and they show elaborate scenes from ancient myths or stories.

WATERCOLOR PAINTING is a technique that uses paints mixed with water. When applied to a canvas or sheet of paper, watercolor paints spread out and form fuzzy edges before drying. The paints can also produce bright, shimmering colors.

WOODBLOCK PRINTING is an old technique that uses carved wooden blocks to make prints. First, the artist will carve a design in reverse on a wooden block. The printer will then fill the block with ink and press it onto a canvas or other surface. Because the image is carved in reverse on the block, it will appear normal on the canvas. Chinese and Japanese artists have made woodblock prints for hundreds of years. These pictures often look "two-dimensional," or flat—somewhat like fancy cartoons!

Answers to the quiz questions

Page 16

The term Nighthawks refers to people who stay up late at night. You can also call these people night owls!

Page 39

In his self-portrait, Jacob Lawrence depicted many of the tools that he used as an artist. For example, you can see the paintbrushes in his hands. Behind the artist are containers of paint—along with metal clamps that he used to attach his canvases to their frames.

Page 42

Jasper Johns painted the outline of a whale on the door, which is meant to represent the giant whale from the American novel *Moby Dick*.

A Library of Congress Control Number is available;
British Library Cataloguing-in-Publication Data:
a catalogue record for this book is available from
the British Library; Deutsche Nationalbibliothek
holds a record of this publication in the Deutsche
Nationalbibliografie; detailed bibliographical data can
be found under: http://dnb.ddb.de.

Picture credits:
Art Institute of Chicago: p. 16-17; Louise Bourgeois
Archive: p. 29; CNAC/MNAM/Dist. RMN/Droits réservés:
p. 23; John Reed: p. 32; Yale University Art Gallery: p. 15;
Artothek, Weilheim: p. 12, p. 10; National Academy
of Design, New York: p. 38-39; bpk: p. 34-35; Hans
Hinz/Artothek: p. 5; Hans Namuth/Center for creative
Photography: p. 33

Front cover: Details taken from works by Cassatt (p. 9),
Johns (p. 42), Homer (p. 5).
Frontispiece: Jasper Johns, *Ventriloquist* (detail)

Prestel books are available worldwide. Please
contact your nearest bookseller or one of the
following addresses for information concerning
your local distributor.

Prestel is a member of Verlagsgruppe Random House
GmbH
Prestel Verlag, Munich

www.prestel.de

Prestel Publishing Ltd.
4, Bloomsbury Place, London WC1A 2QA

Prestel Publishing
900 Broadway, Suite 603, New York, NY 10003

www.prestel.com

Editorial direction: Doris Kutschbach
Edited/copyedited: Cynthia Hall
Picture research: Andrea Jaroni
Design and layout: Michael Schmölzl, agenten.und.
freunde, Munich
Production: Nele Krüger
Art direction: Cilly Klotz
Origination: Reproline Mediadateam, Munich
Printing and binding: Tlačiarne BB, spol. s r.o.
Printed on acid-free paper.

ISBN 978-3-7913-7036-1